Chinese Americans

TRISTAN BOYER BINNS

Heinemann Library
Chicago, Illinois

Customer Service 888-454-2279

Visit our website at www.heinemannlibrary.com

Created by the publishing team at Heinemann Library
Designed by Roslyn Broder
Photo research by Scott Braut
Printed and Bound in the United States by Lake Book Manufacturing, Inc.

07 06 05 04 03
10 9 8 7 6 5 4 3 2 1

Library of Congress Cataloging-in-Publication Data
Boyer Binns, Tristan, 1968-
  Chinese Americans / Tristan Boyer Binns.
    p. cm. -- (We are America)
Summary: An overview of the history and daily lives of Chinese people who immigrated to the United States.
Includes bibliographical references (p.) and index.
  ISBN 1-40340-162-4 (lib. bdg.) -- ISBN 1-40340-417-8 (pbk.)
  1. Chinese Americans--History--Juvenile literature. 2. Chinese Americans--Social life and customs--Juvenile literature. [1. Chinese Americans.] I. Title. II. Series.
  E184.C5 B69 2002
  973'.04951--dc21
                            2002004138

Acknowledgments
The author and publishers are grateful to the following for permission to reproduce copyright material: pp. 4, 5 Courtesy of Dr. David Ho; p. 6 California History Section/California State Library; p. 8 Hawaii State Archives; p. 10 The Bancroft Library/Roy D. Graves Pictorial Collection/University of California; p. 11 Arnold Genthe/Corbis; p. 12 Courtesy of the Central Pacific Railroad Photographic History Museum; p. 13 National Archives and Records Administration; p. 14 Bettmann/Corbis; p. 15 California Historical Society: FN-I8240; p. 16 Herald-Examiner Collection/Los Angeles Public Library; p. 18 Morton Beebe/Corbis; p. 19 © 2001 Kerrick James; p. 20 Ryan Anson/Syracuse Newspapers/The Image Works; p. 21 Ben Schwartz/The Daily Progress/AP/WideWorld Photos; p. 22 Gary Conner/Index Stock Imagery, Inc.; p. 23 Jeffry W. Myers/Corbis; p. 24 David Lassman/Syracuse Newspapers/The Image Works; p. 25 Ron Burda/San Jose Mercury News/KRT/NewsCom; p. 26 Scott Braut/PictureEditor.com; p. 27 David Young-Wolff/PhotoEdit, Inc.; p. 28 Ted Thai/TimePix; p. 29 Time Magazine/TimePix.

Cover photographs provided by Corbis (bck) and Jim Cummins/Taxi/Getty Images

Special thanks to Barry Moreno of the Ellis Island Immigration Museum for his comments in preparation of this book. Tristan Boyer Binns thanks Stephanie Pasternak and Dr. David Ho.

Some quotations and material used in this book come from the following sources. In some cases, quotes have been abridged for clarity: p. 9 *The Life Stories of Undistinguished Americans, As Told by Themselves* by Hamilton Holt (New York: Routledge, 1999); p. 19 *Asian American Experiences in the United States* by Joann F. Lee (Jefferson, N.C.: McFarland & Co., 1991); p. 25 *Our Lives* by Myron Berkman (Palatine, Ill.: Linmore Publishing, 1990); p. 27 *Paper Daughter* by M. Elaine Mar (New York: HarperTrade, 2000).

Some words are shown in bold, **like this.** You can find out what they mean by looking in the glossary.

On the cover of this book, a Chinese-American family is shown. A photo from the 1920s of a street in Chinatown, San Francisco, is shown in the background.

Contents

Coming to the United States

David Ho's father, Paul, wanted a job working with electricity. But he couldn't get the right kind of education in Taiwan to get the job. So, in 1956, Paul left and went to the United States to study. For nine years, David and his mother and brother stayed in Taiwan. Then, in 1965, they took a plane to join Paul in California. David's parents thought the family would have a better life in the United States.

David worked hard at school in Taiwan, an island near the country of China. He is shown above wearing his school uniform.

In the two days it took to get to California, David felt scared and nervous. He was a smart twelve-year-old. Now, he would suddenly not be able to talk with other people because he could not speak English. Like many other people who have **immigrated** to the United States since 1965, David had to learn how to live in his new world quickly.

David's family first lived in a neighborhood in the city of Los Angeles. Then, they moved to a house outside of the city. David became happier living in California as he learned to speak more English.

As a child in Taiwan, I had to work a lot harder than children in America do. I got the habit of being hard-working. After about three months, I learned enough English to say basic things and follow what other kids and teachers were saying.
　　　　　　　　　　　　　　—David Ho

Life in China

Most Chinese people in the 1800s were **peasants.**
A war with Great Britain from 1839 to 1842 ruined
farmland in China. People could not feed their
families because they could not farm. Another war
in China from 1850 to 1864 killed twenty million
Chinese people. Floods and **droughts** also made
Chinese people start looking for other countries
where they could go. Between 1851 and 1882,
many Chinese fathers and sons went to the United
States to work and send money back home.

*News reached China of the **Gold Rush** in California. The
Chinese men on the right in this picture were mining for
gold in California in 1852.*

6

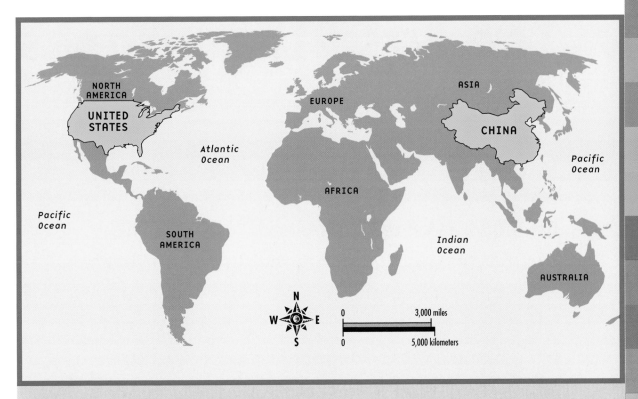

This map shows where China and the United States are located in the world.

Between 1882 and 1965, only a few Chinese people were allowed to come to the United States each year. There was a long war between two groups in China. It ended in 1949. Many of the defeated people fled to Taiwan. After 1965, entire Chinese families **immigrated** to the United States looking for better lives. Most immigrants went to Hong Kong in China and left from there. Many others came from Taiwan.

The **climate** in southeastern China is warm and wet, perfect for growing rice. Most of the first immigrants were farmers and miners used to very hard work.

The First Immigrants

Between 1851 and 1882, about 300,000 Chinese people came to the United States. By mining, farming, fishing, or working in factories, Chinese men could earn more money in the United States than they could in China. A lot of them hoped to go back to China when they had made enough money. Most Chinese people had to borrow money to get to the United States. They paid it back by working for many years. It was very hard for the men to leave China.

Chinese immigrants like these on their way to Hawaii in 1900 usually had to bring and cook their own food.

Chinese Immigration to the United States

These are some of the cities and states that the first Chinese immigrants came to in the United States and still live in today.

It usually took one to two months to get to California from China by ship. The **immigrants** had to travel 7,000 miles (11,265 kilometers) across the Pacific Ocean. The ships were very crowded, and the sailors and the immigrants did not usually speak the same language. Most ships came to a **port** like San Francisco, California, where the Chinese men began their new lives.

> All my life I had been used to sleeping on a board bunk with a wooden pillow, and I found the **steamer's** bunk very uncomfortable, because it was so soft.
>
> —Chinese immigrant Lee Chew, 1882

The Early Years

Many Chinese people stayed and worked in the city of San Francisco. They started the first **Chinatown** there. Over time, Chinatowns grew in other cities, like Chicago and New York. Most of the Chinese people living in the United States didn't have family members with them. They wanted to spend as little money as possible, so they lived in **dormitories.** They were often not allowed to rent places anywhere else in the city.

This picture shows what San Francisco's Chinatown looked like in 1898.

In American Chinatowns, people dressed as they had in China. They ate the same kinds of foods, and the stores sold the same kind of things as they did in China. This family is shown in San Francisco in 1904.

Special Chinese **associations** were also formed. Clan associations, or family associations, were made up of people who had the same family names and backgrounds. District associations were made up of people who came from the same counties in China. Both groups helped Chinese people find jobs and places to live. The groups also helped Chinese people deal with the **prejudice** of some Americans.

Between 1790 and 1943, Chinese people could not become U.S. citizens unless they were born in the United States.

Old Ways of Working in a New World

Many Chinese **immigrants** had been miners in China. They knew how to get the small bits of gold left behind by other miners in California. When gold was found deep inside of rocks, Chinese people knew how to get the gold out. But because they were Chinese, they were paid only half of what other American miners were paid. A law was also passed in 1850 that made Chinese miners and other immigrants pay a tax in order to mine.

Chinese men helped build the railroads. The tracks had to be built through mountains and valleys. It was hard work, and many Chinese people did it very well.

*Chinese people opened **laundries** because many people in the West had no way to clean their clothes. The laundries didn't cost much money to open, and cleaning clothes was a job that was easy to learn.*

Chinese people also taught others how to farm in California. Most of the land was wet and hard to farm, but the Chinese people had farmed on land like it in China. They knew how to grow fruit and vegetables. Chinese people also helped start the fishing **industry** in the United States. Many had lived and worked in fishing villages in China.

Lue Gim Gong moved to the United States from China in 1872, when he was twelve. He grew different types of oranges until he found a new kind that grew well in Florida. He helped to make Florida a successful fruit-growing state.

Immigration Ban

When Chinese people started coming to the United States, they were sometimes treated unfairly. In most places, Chinese people were not allowed to become citizens, marry white Americans, or buy homes. Because Chinese **immigrants** agreed to work for less pay than others did, some people thought the immigrants would take away all of the jobs. People began to dislike the Chinese because of this and wanted them to leave the United States.

*On October 31, 1880, Chinese people and their businesses were attacked in Denver, Colorado, in the city's **Chinatown** area. This drawing shows what the attacks probably looked like.*

This photo shows women waiting at Angel Island. All immigrants who came to San Francisco from 1910 to 1940 had to go to the island. They were looked at and asked questions, and they often had to stay for a long time.

In 1882, the United States government passed a law. It said that no more Chinese workers could come to the United States. Chinese people could only come to the United States if they had parents or children already there. Many Chinese children were still sent to work in the United States. They claimed to have parents in the United States, but they really did not. In 1943, the immigration ban was lifted, but only 105 Chinese people could go to the United States each year.

More than 14,000 Chinese Americans fought for the United States in World War Two from 1941 to 1945.

More Immigrants

In 1965, the United States government decided that 20,000 Chinese could enter the United States each year. Women came to join their husbands and sons, and entire families also **immigrated.** Many of the new immigrants had gone to college and had good jobs in China. They were looking for opportunities they didn't have at home. Other immigrants were poor and had no special skills. They thought they could live a better life in the United States.

The Chang family came to the United States in 1962 from Hong Kong. Mr. Chang had worked for the U.S. Army.

Time Line

1851   Thousands of Chinese people come to the United States during the **Gold Rush.**

1882–1943 Most Chinese not allowed to immigrate to the U.S.

1943   Only 105 Chinese people are allowed to immigrate to the U.S. each year.

1965   Immigration law changed to let 20,000 Chinese people immigrate each year.

2000   More than 41,000 Chinese people immigrate to the U.S.

They called the flight. All of a sudden I just didn't want to go! I wasn't ever going to see [my grandmother] again, and so I grabbed onto the railing and I refused to let go. I was hanging on and I ran back to my grandmother. We went on the plane and I still cried for a long time.

—Mai Lin, who came from Taiwan in 1977 when she was ten

Even though some Chinese immigrants were treated badly in the past, the Chinese phrase for "America" is *Mei Guo,* which means "beautiful country."

Settling Down

Even today, Chinese **immigrants** still arrive in the United States every year. Many of the new immigrants move to be near family or friends. They live in many places, from Kansas to Colorado and Seattle to New York. Some choose to live in areas where no one else is Chinese. Others move to **Chinatown** areas in cities across the country.

In Chinatowns in the United States, signs are usually written in the Chinese language.

About 100,000 people live in San Francisco's Chinatown area. The main street there, Grant Avenue, is shown in this picture.

In 2000, about 164,000 people lived in New York City's Chinatown. In places where many Chinese Americans live, there are family and district **associations.** These are clubs where people go for celebrations, like Chinese New Year. They meet other Chinese people. New immigrants can also learn more about the United States.

Being in Chinatown is like being back in the village in China. Everyday I am with Chinese people, I speak the language, and the food is the same, so it's not like being away at all. It's not unless I go into the country that I really feel I am in America.

—Chin Cai Ping, who came from China in 1984

Homes and Families

Like all Americans, Chinese Americans move into many different kinds of homes. In cities, they live in apartments. Other Chinese Americans buy houses outside of the city. Some share houses with relatives. Some Chinese-American families eat mostly Chinese food and speak only Chinese at home.

*Chinese-American children often learn Chinese **traditions** from family members. This boy is singing a traditional Chinese song.*

This six-year-old girl from China became a United States citizen in 2001 with the help of her parents.

For some Chinese **immigrants,** learning English can be hard. Children often learn English more quickly than their parents do because they need it in school. Many older immigrants learn English because of their work. Some live in Chinese neighborhoods and work with Chinese people, so they do not learn English right away. Others already know how to speak English before they immigrate.

> Certain American foods I didn't like a lot. The vegetables tasted terrible. The Chinese cook vegetables much better. I liked hamburgers, steaks, spaghetti.
> —Sidney Chang, who came from Taiwan in 1968 when he was six

Working and Playing

Many Chinese Americans have special skills, like shipbuilding or carpentry, and they want to use these skills in the United States. Sometimes they have problems speaking English, and this makes it difficult to get the type of jobs they want. Many Chinese people learn English, start small businesses, or go to school in the United States. Some Chinese Americans get jobs in **high-tech industries.**

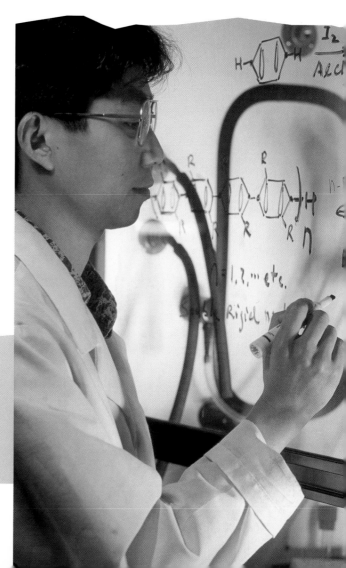

This Chinese American works in a laboratory in Los Angeles.

These Chinese-American kids are shown playing with friends from their school in Seattle, Washington.

Like children everywhere, Chinese-American children sometimes have to work to help earn money for their families. They might also help with **family businesses.** Like all kids, Chinese Americans like to play with their friends. They teach their American friends **traditional** games like **mah-jongg.**

I. M. Pei is a famous Chinese American who has designed buildings all over the world. He was born in 1917 and moved to the United States in 1935. One of his most famous buildings is a glass-pyramid entrance to the Louvre Museum in Paris, France.

Going to School

Like all children in the United States, Chinese-American children go to school, even if they haven't been in the country that long. If they are new **immigrants,** school can be hard. Sometimes, there are other Chinese students to help them get used to the school.

These Chinese-American kids from New York are making a painting of a village in China.

This student in California gets help from his teacher while he learns how to write the Chinese alphabet.

Many Chinese-American families feel that it is important to keep and learn **traditions** from China. Some children learn to speak and write the Chinese language at special schools in which they study Chinese writing, history, geography, or music. Many of these schools have their own bands, choirs, or dance groups.

I didn't understand anyone speaking English, and I could not speak English. Sometimes the American people asked me questions. I just said, "I don't know" and "I can't speak English."

—Mike Yim, who came from China in the 1980s when he was a teenager

Celebrations

Chinese Americans celebrate many special holidays. Chinese New Year is a two-week-long festival that is celebrated in January or February. People have parades and watch fireworks. They honor family members and have special meals, like vegetable dishes that take a long time to make. For good luck, children are given money wrapped in red paper called *li shee*.

*This is a Chinese New Year's celebration in New York City's **Chinatown.** Children and adults carry a long dragon made out of paper and plastic.*

*These Chinese-American girls are wearing **traditional** Chinese clothing as they perform in a parade for Chinese New Year's.*

The dragon head is six feet tall and really scary. It has big mean eyes and whiskers everywhere.

—Elaine Mar, talking about the dragon-dance parade. Elaine came to the United States from China in 1972, when she was six years old.

In September, Chinese Americans celebrate the Moon Festival to honor the full moon. People eat moon cakes, which are made of sweet dough filled with fruit or seeds. The cakes look like full moons. Of course, Chinese Americans celebrate other holidays, too, like Christmas and Easter.

Doctor David Ho

Dr. Ho works in this laboratory to find out more about AIDS.

David Ho became a doctor. He works to learn about the **virus** that makes people sick with **AIDS.** He is helping to stop it with medicine. In 1996, *Time* magazine gave David an award because his work helped sick people. David thinks coming to the United States helped him to be a success. He learned that he could do difficult things, even when they seemed impossible.

Like many Chinese Americans, David feels that he has Chinese and American **values.** He and his wife raised their children to understand Chinese language and history. They think that having a close family is important. They might enjoy celebrating Chinese New Year more than New Year's Day, January 1, but they are proud to be American, too.

This is the cover of the Time *magazine in which David was given the Man of the Year award.*

Chinese Immigration Chart

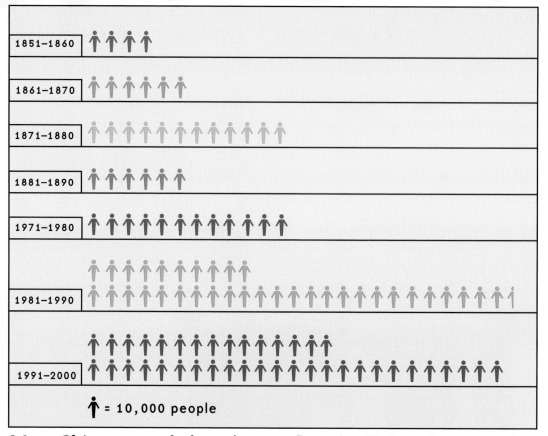

1851–1860	🚶🚶🚶🚶
1861–1870	🚶🚶🚶🚶🚶🚶
1871–1880	🚶🚶🚶🚶🚶🚶🚶🚶🚶🚶🚶
1881–1890	🚶🚶🚶🚶🚶🚶
1971–1980	🚶🚶🚶🚶🚶🚶🚶🚶🚶🚶🚶🚶
1981–1990	🚶🚶🚶🚶🚶🚶🚶🚶🚶
	🚶🚶🚶🚶🚶🚶🚶🚶🚶🚶🚶🚶🚶🚶🚶🚶🚶🚶🚶🚶🚶🚶🚶🚶🚶🚶
1991–2000	🚶🚶🚶🚶🚶🚶🚶🚶🚶🚶🚶🚶🚶🚶🚶🚶🚶
	🚶🚶🚶🚶🚶🚶🚶🚶🚶🚶🚶🚶🚶🚶🚶🚶🚶🚶🚶🚶🚶🚶🚶🚶🚶🚶🚶🚶🚶

🚶 = 10,000 people

*More Chinese people **immigrated** to the United States in the 1980s and 1990s than ever before.*

Source: U.S. Immigration and Naturalization Service

More Books to Read

Bloom, Barbara Lee. *The Chinese-Americans (Immigrants in America).* San Diego: Lucent Books, 2002.

Kite, Lorien. *We Came to North America: The Chinese.* New York: Crabtree Publishing, 2000.

Olson, Kay Melchisedech. *Chinese Immigrants, 1850-1900.* Mankato, Minn.: Blue Earth Books, 2001.

Raatma, Lucia. *Chinese Americans.* Chanhassen, Minn.: The Child's World, 2002.

Glossary

AIDS deadly disease in which the human body cannot fight off infection

association group of people who have something in common and work together toward a goal

Chinatown area in a city where a large number of Chinese people live and own businesses

climate typical weather of a place over a number of years

dormitory building where many people live in rooms that are usually small

drought long period of time with little or no rain

family business business owned and run by members of a family

Gold Rush time from 1848 to 1859 when gold was found in California. People from all over the world went there to try to get rich.

high-tech shortened version of "high technology," which is a science that uses complex electronic machines and devices

immigrate to come to a country to live there for a long time. A person who immigrates is an immigrant.

industry business

laundry business that cleans people's clothing and other items

mah-jongg Chinese game that is like dominoes

peasant person who lives by fishing or farming on a small area of land and who does not own many things

port city near water where ships dock and leave from

prejudice unfair belief about a person based on what they look like or where they come from

steamer ship powered by a steam engine. Also called a steamship.

tradition belief or practice handed down through the years from one generation to the next

value what people think is something special or important in life

virus tiny, nonliving thing inside your body that can make you sick

Index